WHAT'S IT LIKE TO BE A

BABY
POLAR BEAR?

Published in the United States in 1998 by
The Millbrook Press, Inc.
2 Old New Milford Road
Brookfield, Connecticut 06804

First published in Great Britain in 1998 by
Belitha Press Limited
London House, Great Eastern Wharf
Parkgate Road, London SW11 4NQ

Editor: Honor Head
Designers: Hayley Cove, Victoria Monks
Illustrator: Graham Rosewarne
Consultants: Sally Morgan and Wendy Body

Cataloging-in-Publication data is on file at the
Library of Congress

Printed in Belgium

Photo credits: B & C Alexander: p. 13; BBC Natural
History Unit: pp. 6, 15 (top), 20 (Thomas D.
Mangelsen), 26 (Martha Holmes), 28 (bottom) (Jeff
Foott); Bruce Coleman Ltd.: p. 19 (Fred Bruemmer);
FLPA: cover, pp. 4 (bottom), 24 (top), 27 (Norbert
Rosing/Silvestris), 11, 31 (Silvestris), 16 (R. van
Nostrand); Getty Images: pp. 9 (Kathy Bushue), 12
(Mickey Sexton), 22-23 (Bryn Campbell), 28 (top) (Jeff
Foott); NHPA: pp. 18, 24 (bottom) (Gerard Lacz);
Photo Researchers Inc./OSF: pp. 10, 15 (bottom) (Dan
Guravich); Planet Earth Pictures: pp. 4 (top), 8 (Nikita
Ovsyanikov), 4 (bottom).

WHAT'S IT LIKE TO BE A

BABY POLAR BEAR?

by Honor Head

Illustrated by
Graham Rosewarne

The Millbrook Press
Brookfield, Connecticut

There are lots of
different types of bears—
brown bears, black bears,
and polar bears. Bears live
all around the world.

A baby bear is called a cub. This book is about what it's like to be a polar bear cub. When you read this book, imagine that you are a baby polar bear....

You live in a cold and snowy place called the Arctic. Before you were born your mother dug a hole in the snow. This hole is called a den. In the den you are warm and safe. You are born during the winter months.

When you are born you are the size of a guinea pig. You are blind and don't have any teeth. When you are hungry you snuggle in your mother's fur and drink her milk.

You leave the den
when it is spring.
Now you are about
three months old.

When you first come out of the den you are still very small. Sometimes a male polar bear might attack you. Your mother makes loud noises to scare away enemies. At night you still sleep in the den for safety.

You and your brothers and sisters stay close to your mother as you get used to the sunlight. You make lots of noises. You hiss, squeal, and make little rumbling sounds in your throat.

When you are small
your fur is very white.
Your mother licks you
to help keep you clean.

You may be the only cub born, or you may have one or two sisters and brothers born at the same time. You do not live with other bears. When you are a baby you live only with your brothers, sisters, and mother.

You love to play with your brothers and sisters. You enjoy tumbling and rolling in the snow.

When you are old enough your mother takes you on a journey to the sea. If the sea is far away, it can be a very long walk.

Sometimes your mother carries you on her back through deep snow and water.

When you
reach the sea
your mother
teaches you
to swim.

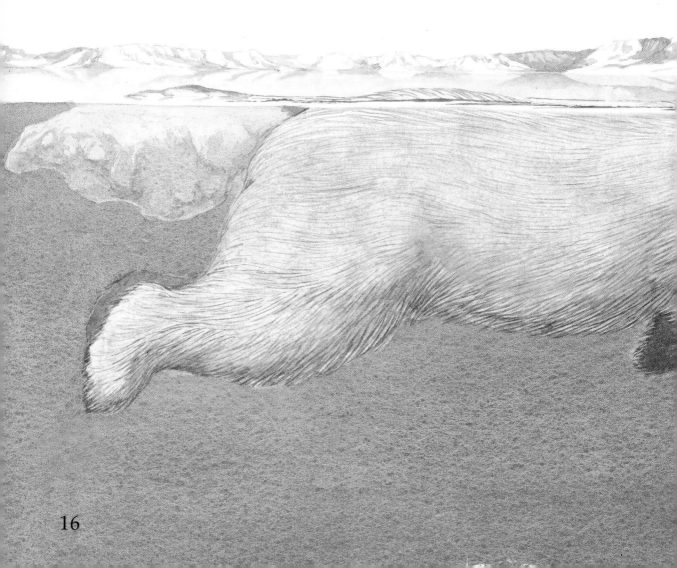

You swim by paddling your front legs. Your back legs stay still. You can dive and swim under the water, too. You close your nostrils and keep your eyes open underwater. Your front feet are slightly webbed, like a duck's.

You spend most of your time searching for food. Sometimes you go for days without eating. You have very long, sharp claws. You use your claws to catch and hold fish.

In the spring and summer you dig in the snow for grass and seaweed. You creep up on birds.

Your favorite food is seal. If you see a seal floating on a piece of ice, you swim up to it through the water. Sometimes you sit next to a hole in the snow and ice and wait for a seal to come up for air. Then you grab it.

You can smell a seal even when it is under the ice.
Your mother teaches you to creep up to where the seal
is. Then you jump up and down to break the ice and
catch the seal.

Your white coat makes
you difficult to see
against the snow.
This means that you
can hunt animals
without being seen.

But you have a shiny black nose. Some people say that when you go hunting you cover your nose with your paw to hide it.

When you have eaten, you clean yourself by rolling in the snow or splashing in water.

In between meals you like to sleep. On warm days you like to stretch out in the sun with your feet in the air. You can sleep in any position.

You have a thick layer of fat underneath your fur. This keeps you warm in the snow and icy waters. You have thick fur on the bottom of your feet to keep you from slipping on the ice.

Y̶ou usually walk on all fours like other types of bears.

S̶ometimes you stand up on your back legs. This helps you to sniff the air and to see what is in the distance.

On cold days you cover your nose. This helps to keep you warm. When there is a snowstorm you curl up and sleep through it.

You may stay like this for several days and get covered with snow. When the storm passes you wake up and shake off the snow.

You will leave your mother when you are about two and a half years old. If you are a male, you will live by yourself.

If you are a female polar bear you will have your first set of cubs when you are about four or five years old. When one set of cubs has grown up and left home, you have another set. You live to the age of about 30.

INDEX OF USEFUL WORDS

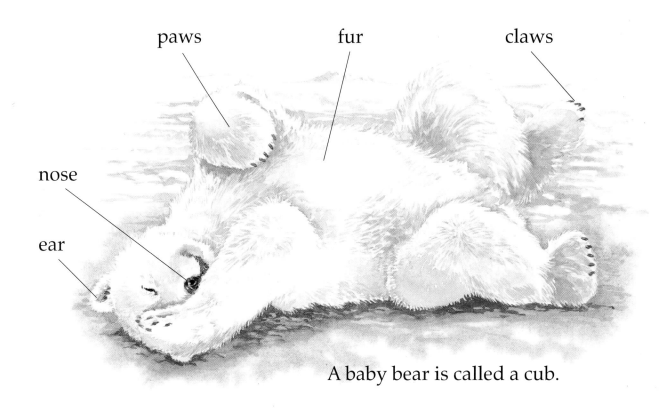

paws   fur   claws

nose

ear

A baby bear is called a cub.